The Apache

D1223637

MARK FRIEDMAN
AND PETER BENOIT

Children's Press®
An Imprint of Scholastic Inc.
New York Toronto London Auckland Sydney
Mexico City New Delhi Hong Kong
Danbury, Connecticut

DISCARD

Content Consultant

Scott Manning Stevens, PhD
Director, McNickle Center
Newberry Library
Chicago, Illinois

Library of Congress Cataloging-in-Publication Data

Friedman, Mark, 1963–
  The Apache/Mark Friedman and Peter Benoit.
     p. cm.—(A true book)
  Includes bibliographical references and index.
  ISBN-13: 978-0-531-20769-7 (lib. bdg.)   978-0-531-29311-9 (pbk.)
  ISBN-10: 0-531-20769-2 (lib. bdg.)   0-531-29311-4 (pbk.)
  1. Apache Indians—Juvenile literature. I. Benoit, Peter, 1955– II. Title. III. Series.
   E99.A6F85 2011
   979.004'9725—dc22   2010049078

All rights reserved. Published in 2011 by Children's Press, an imprint of Scholastic Inc.
Printed in China 62
SCHOLASTIC, CHILDREN'S PRESS, A TRUE BOOK and associated logos are trademarks and/or registered trademarks of Scholastic Inc.

1 2 3 4 5 6 7 8 9 10 R 19 18 17 16 15 14 13 12 11

Find the Truth!

Everything you are about to read is true *except* for one of the sentences on this page.

Which one is **TRUE**?

T or F   Almost all Apache warriors were men.

T or F   An Apache woman joined her husband's family when she married.

Find the answers in this book.

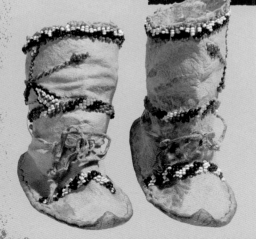

Contents

THE **BIG** TRUTH!

Apache Warriors

Geronimo was not only
a warrior, he was also
considered a healer.

Geronimo

4

Apache ceremony

3 Geronimo

4 The Apache People Today

A buckskin pouch with beadwork

Canada

United States

Colorado

Arizona

New Mexico

Oklahoma

Texas

Atlantic Ocean

Pacific Ocean

Gulf of Mexico

Mexico

This map shows where the Apache lived in the 1800s and where their reservations are today.

LEGEND

Apache territory in the 1800s

Apache today

N W E S

CHAPTER 1

The Apache Indians

The Apache (uh-PAH-chee) Indians are a Native American group that has been living in North America for hundreds of years. The Apache have lived in what is now Texas, New Mexico, Arizona, Oklahoma, and northern Mexico. People of Apache heritage now make their homes in many places across the United States. Today's Apache include the Western Apache, the Chiricahua (cheer-uh-COW-uh), the Jicarilla (hee-ka-REE-ah), the Mescalero (mess-ka-LAIR-oh), the Plains Apache, and the Lipan (li-PON) people.

← Many Apache prefer to call themselves *Ndéé* (NUH-deh), which means "the people."

Hard work and cooperation were vital to the survival of Apache families.

Family Groups

In the past, Apache families lived close together. As a family grew, it remained a closely knit group with a male leader who made all the decisions. Families sometimes banded together to fight an enemy or to go on a journey. Other times, families had different goals. For example, one family might make peace with a neighboring town while another family made war against it.

Members of the Family

Apache families remained together as the children grew. Several generations of young and old people from the same family—grandparents, aunts, uncles, and cousins—lived together. Adult children who were not married would live with the family. As a daughter grew to be an adult and got married, her husband joined her family.

If a husband or wife died, any children remained with their mother's family.

A recently married Apache couple

Food From Nature

Apache foods came from the land on which the people lived or from the animals of the land. The Apache ate cactus, berries, and root vegetables such as potatoes. Some Apache families farmed the land to grow corn and other crops. The main source of food was wild animals. Apache boys were taught to be hunters from a very early age. The Apache hunted bison (buffalo), wild turkey, bear, and even mountain lion to eat.

Prickly pear cactus fruit was collected in the autumn. The flesh of these fruits is often sweet and juicy.

Bison

The bison was an important animal to the Apache people. Bison meat was their main food. They also made use of bison hides. The Apache wore clothes made of bison skin. They used bison skins as blankets and tents. They made tools out of bison bones.

Bison can run at speeds of more than 30 miles per hour (48 kilometers per hour).

G.W.BACKHOU

Teepees

Some Apache people lived in teepees. Teepees were cone-shaped tents made of birch bark or buffalo skins. They had an opening at the top and flaps to let smoke out. These allowed people to cook over an open fire in the teepee. Teepees were easy to set up, take down, and move.

Apache teepees were lightweight dwellings.

Wickiups could be built in a matter of hours.

Two Apache women in front of a wickiup. The structures were often covered with bits of cloth or old clothing.

Wickiups

Other Apache people lived in **wickiups** (WIK-ee-ups). These dome-shaped houses were about 7 feet (2 meters) tall. To build a wickiup, people drove poles of oak or willow into the ground and tied them together with strands of yucca leaves. They covered the poles with bunches of brush or stiff grass tied together. A smoke hole was created in the roof so smoke from the fire could escape.

Some Apache baskets were woven tightly enough to hold water.

The Apache were expert basket makers. They did not create much pottery.

Apache Art

Apache men and women created beautiful works of art by weaving. Apache women made baskets to carry and store food and other things. They created the baskets from reeds and leaves of plants. They wove interesting shapes or animals in their detailed designs. The women used flowers to dye the baskets different colors.

Beads and Beading

Another form of Apache art was beading. Apache women made beads out of turquoise, amber, ivory, bones, and many other materials. The Apache used beads for trading and to decorate clothing, pouches, and other everyday items. People today continue to admire the beautiful artwork that the Apache created hundreds of years ago.

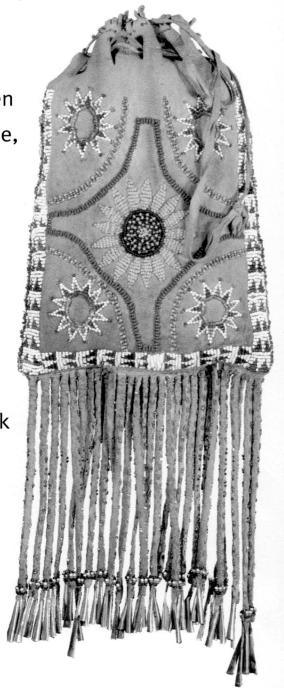

This pouch features beautiful beadwork, including a sunflower design near the center.

15

Language

As a group, the Apache people are bound together by the **Athabascan** (ath-uh-BAS-can) language family. Many other Native American nations, including the Navajo people, speak a language from this language family. The Western Apache, for example, spoke somewhat differently from other Apache groups.

The Western Apache word for *owl* is *búh* (BOO).

The Apache feared owls. An owl's hoots were thought to be a ghost's voice speaking the Apache language.

An Apache elder sits outside her home. Elders used storytelling to communicate the history and traditions of their people to younger generations.

Ways to Communicate

The Apache had different ways of communicating. They used their own spoken language to tell stories and talk among themselves. Often they signed with their hands to trade with outsiders.

To communicate to other Apache over a long distance, the Apache used smoke signals. Puffs of smoke were combined differently to send different messages. Two puffs meant "All is well." Three puffs in a row meant "Trouble! Send help!"

Francisco Vásquez de Coronado explored the Southwest in search of gold, which he did not find.

CHAPTER 2

Apache History

The first Apache came to today's American Southwest hundreds of years ago. They may have come from present-day Canada between 1100 and the early 1500s. The Apache were **nomads**. They moved in search of food and water.

Spanish explorer Francisco Vásquez de Coronado was likely the first European to meet the Apache, in 1541. He called them "dog nomads" because they used dogs to pull their belongings on sleds called **travois** (tra-VOY).

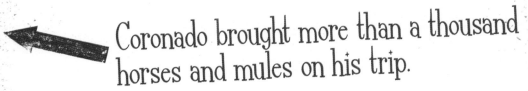

Coronado brought more than a thousand horses and mules on his trip.

The Apache were expert riders.

The Spanish introduced horses to the Apache.

The Spanish Bring Change

Coronado was one of many explorers from Spain who traveled through America during the 1500s and later. The Spanish wanted to claim new lands for Spain. They built small villages called **missions**. The Spanish living in the missions tried to **convert** the Indians to Christianity. The Spanish brought European diseases with them, which killed many Native Americans. Contact with the Spanish forever changed Native American ways of life.

Years of Conflict

The biggest change was that the Apache entered into conflict that lasted for hundreds of years. Some Apache groups were friendly with the Spanish. Other Apache groups fought with the outsiders. These Apache raided horses, tools, and food from the Spanish. Spanish soldiers fought back. The battles were violent, and many people died on both sides.

Spanish colonizers and, later, American settlers reduced Apache territory, limiting the mobility of nomadic Apache groups.

The Mexican-American War

The Apache had made enemies in Mexico by attacking villages. Throughout the early 1800s, Apache-Mexican battles cost many lives.

Then, in 1845, the United States claimed Texas. Mexico insisted that Texas was part of its lands. This conflict led to the Mexican-American War (1846–1848).

Nearly all U.S. soldiers in the Mexican-American War were volunteers.

Santa Fe, shown here, was one of many towns and areas that fell under U.S. control after the United States and Mexico signed a peace treaty.

Peace Treaties

The Apache in Texas and northern Mexico sided with the United States during the war. The Apache allowed U.S. soldiers to travel through their land to get to the battlegrounds in Mexico.

The United States signed a peace **treaty** with Mexico in 1848. In the treaty, the United States got all of today's Texas, California, Utah, and Nevada, and most of today's Arizona and New Mexico. Mexico got $15 million from the United States.

The California gold rush lasted from 1848 to 1853.

Only a small number of seekers ever found gold.

Gold Rush!

For a time, the Apache and the Americans had a good relationship. It began to fall apart in the early 1850s. That was when thousands of Americans were traveling west as part of the California gold rush. They were hoping to get rich mining for gold. Many stopped in New Mexico and Arizona. The miners and other settlers from the East tried to move onto lands that the Native Americans called home.

Conflicts With Americans

In the early 1850s, gold miners captured Apache chief Mangas Coloradas, tied him to a tree, and beat him. It was one of several violent conflicts between the Apache and the miners. One side would attack the other side's village. Then the other side would attack in revenge. By the mid-1850s, the U.S. Army got involved and fought against the Apache. By then, the once-good relationship had ended.

Some Apaches tried to cut off traffic through their lands, attacking wagon trains that passed by.

Cochise and Bascom

On February 4, 1861, an American army officer named George Bascom tried to arrest Cochise, an Apache chief. Cochise was accused of kidnapping the son of a Mexican rancher. Cochise was innocent, but Bascom didn't believe him. Cochise escaped from the army camp and captured several white people as **hostages**. In return, Bascom held Cochise's relatives as hostages. The two sides failed to make peace. Each man, in the end, killed all his hostages.

Cochise

Cochise was at least 5 inches (13 centimeters) taller than the average Apache.

The Apache Wars

This alarming event started the period known as the Apache Wars. Cochise joined together with other Apache chiefs, including Mangas Coloradas. They staged bloody attacks on the white settlers and U.S. Army troops in their region. The battles of the Apache Wars cost thousands of lives, including that of Mangas Coloradas in 1863.

Apache warriors often fought using guns they acquired through raids or trade with settlers and soldiers.

Forced Onto Reservations

As the years passed, the U.S. government forced Apache people and other Native American groups to move out of their homes. U.S. soldiers took the Indians to live on **reservations**. These are areas where Native Americans of many different nations were forced to live. Meanwhile, white settlers took over their land.

The Apache Wars lasted a quarter-century.

Timeline of the Apache in the U.S.

1846–1848

The Apache side with the United States during the Mexican-American War.

1861

The Cochise-Bascom conflict starts the Apache Wars.

Surrender

Everything changed in September 1886. After chasing the Apache chief Geronimo for weeks, the U.S. Army finally trapped him at Skeleton Canyon, Arizona. He and his band had fought with white settlers for years. Now cornered, Geronimo **surrendered**. It was the end of the Apache Wars.

Many defeated Apache warriors, including Geronimo, were put in prison in Florida, far from home. Many died there of disease. Geronimo lived another 13 years but was never allowed to return to Arizona, his home.

1886
Geronimo is captured, ending the Apache Wars.

21st century
More than 100,000 people in the United States are at least part Apache.

Apache Warriors

The Apache people spent hundreds of years fighting against the Spanish, Mexicans, Americans, and other Native Americans. They fought to protect their homes, their families, and their land. Through the years, several famous warriors rose up to lead the Apache people.

An Apache
war party

Mangas Coloradas

(circa 1795–1863) was chief of Apache groups in New Mexico. He led Apache attacks against Mexico and made peace with the United States during the Mexican-American War. U.S. soldiers killed him in 1863, which led to increased warfare and Apache distrust of the United States.

Cochise

(circa 1812–1874) was the main Apache warrior chief from 1861 to 1871.

Geronimo

(1829–1909) was the most famous Apache chief. He led attacks on American settlers from 1858 to 1886. He was famous for escaping capture as if by a miracle. (See the next chapter.)

Lozen

Most Apache warriors were men, but Lozen (circa 1840–1890) was a rare woman warrior. According to legend, she could predict what the enemy was going to do.

The mix of Native American and European cultures is seen in this photo of Geronimo wearing a horned headdress and grasping a pistol.

CHAPTER 3

Geronimo

Geronimo was the most famous and most feared Apache warrior. His name at birth was Goyathlay (goy-ANHK-lah), meaning "one who yawns." When Goyathlay was a young man in 1858, some 400 Mexican soldiers came to his camp while he and the other Apache men were away. The Mexicans murdered his wife, three children, and mother. Along with the chief Cochise, Goyathlay spent years seeking revenge for his family's deaths.

Geronimo was a member of the Chiricahua Apache.

Goyathlay Becomes Geronimo

In one battle against the Mexicans, Goyathlay attacked the Mexican soldiers over and over again. It seemed that he was not affected by the bullets being fired at him. The soldiers were so astonished they said prayers to the Christian saint Jerome, or *Jeronimo* in Spanish. After that, Goyathlay was always known as Geronimo.

Saint Jerome translated the Bible from Hebrew and Greek to Latin.

Geronimo's Powers

The Apache believed Geronimo had many powers. Some people said he could see into the future. He escaped capture numerous times, often in mysterious ways. He once ran into a cave in New Mexico's Robledo Mountains to escape from soldiers. The soldiers waited outside the cave for hours, but he never came out. He had somehow escaped, yet no one could find another entrance to the cave.

Some people believed that Geronimo could walk without leaving tracks.

The Most Powerful Leader

Geronimo had many loyal followers. He called on them to attack Mexican towns almost constantly. Later, they attacked white settlements and U.S. Army camps across New Mexico, Arizona, and western Texas. When Geronimo surrendered to the Americans, the Apache lost their most powerful leader.

A stone monument was built in 1934 near the site of Geronimo's surrender, in memory of the event.

Geronimooooo!

Geronimo and his horse once leaped from Medicine Bluff, near Fort Sill, Oklahoma. It is a rock cliff 310 feet (94 m) high. Nobody knows how it happened, but he survived the fall. Some people said he shouted his name as he jumped. Whether or not this is true, this legend made its way into a 1939 movie about Geronimo. Ever since then, people who are taking big jumps from high or dangerous places sometimes shout "Geronimo!"

Geronimo on horseback in Arizona. Apache boys began learning to ride and care for horses around age seven.

An Apache girl is painted with a mixture of clay and cornmeal as she takes part in a ceremony celebrating her passage into womanhood.

CHAPTER 4

The Apache People Today

Many years have passed since the warrior days of the Apache. Native Americans are proud of the bravery and strength shown by their ancestors. They also still feel the pain of the ways in which they were mistreated by Americans in the past. But as a people, the Apache are interested in moving forward and building a strong future.

 Today, about 15,000 people speak Apache languages.

Where the Apache Live

Today, about 57,000 Americans call themselves Apache. Six Apache groups live in different areas of the American Southwest. The Mescalero Apache and the Jicarilla live in New Mexico. The Chiricahua live in New Mexico, Arizona, and Oklahoma. The Lipan Apache live in New Mexico and Texas. The Western Apache live in Arizona, and the Plains Apache live in Oklahoma.

The small town of Peridot is located on the San Carlos Reservation in Arizona.

Apache children on horseback on Arizona's Fort Apache Indian Reservation

Tourism provides money and jobs for many Apache on reservations.

Modern Reservations

Some Apache live in towns and cities all across the United States. But many Apache people live on reservations in southwestern states. Today's reservations are different from the reservations of the past. In the 1800s, the government began forcing Native Americans onto reservations against their will. Today, Apache people live on reservations by choice.

Controlling Their Own Future

Apache reservations are similar to small nations. They have their own governments, businesses, police, and schools, all run by the Apache. Most Apache speak English, but some still know the language of their ancestors. For today's Apache, modern life is a journey during which they celebrate their past and work toward a promising future. ★

Some Apaches work as firefighters. They help combat forest fires for the U.S. Forest Service.

Name most Apache prefer to call themselves: Ndéé, which means "the people"

Year that Coronado first met the Apache: 1541

Length of the Apache Wars: 25 years

Year that Geronimo surrendered: 1886

Number of Apache groups today: 6

Number of Apache Americans in 2000: About 57,000

Number of Americans who call themselves at least part Apache Indian in 2000: More than 100,000

Bison

Did you find the truth?

T Almost all Apache warriors were men.

F An Apache woman joined her husband's family when she married.

Resources

Books

Behnke, Alison. *The Apaches*. Minneapolis: Lerner Publications Co., 2007.

Gendell, Megan. *The Spanish Missions of Texas*. New York: Children's Press, 2010.

Lyon, Robin. *The Spanish Missions of Arizona*. New York: Children's Press, 2010.

McIntosh, Kenneth. *Apache*. North American Indians Today. Philadelphia: Mason Crest Publishers, 2004.

Sonneborn, Liz. *The Apache*. New York: Franklin Watts, 2005.

Welch, Catherine A. *Geronimo*. Minneapolis: Lerner Publications, 2004.

Worth, Richard. *The Apache: A Proud People*. Berkeley Heights, NJ: Enslow, 2005.

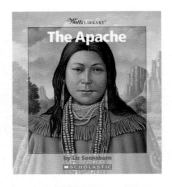

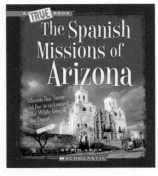

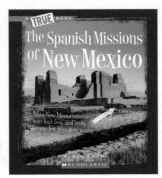

Organizations and Web Sites

Geronimo: His Own Story
http://odur.let.rug.nl/~usa/B/geronimo/geronixx
Read Geronimo's life story told in his own words.

Find out about the governments and people of these nations:
Chiricahua Apache Nde Nation
www.chiricahuaapache.org
Jicarilla Apache Nation
http://jicarillaonline.com
Mescalero Apache Tribe
www.mescaleroapache.org
White Mountain Apache Tribe
www.wmat.nsn.us

Places to Visit

Fort Apache Historic Park
P.O. Box 628
Fort Apache, AZ 85926
(928) 338-4625
www.wmat.nsn.us/
fortapachepark.htm
Explore Apache history and customs at the site of a U.S. Army outpost from the Apache Wars period.

Living Desert Zoo and Gardens State Park
Annual Mescal Roast
P.O. Box 100
Carlsbad, NM 88221
(575) 887-5516
www.emnrd.state.nm.us/PRD/MescalRoast.htm
Get details about the Mescalero Apache four-day celebration held every May.

Important Words

Athabascan (a-tha-BAS-kin) the family of Native American languages that includes Apache

convert (kuhn-VURT)—to change someone's beliefs

hostages (HOSS-tij-iz)—people who are captured and held as prisoners

missions (MISH-uhnz)—villages built to settle the land and convert the local people

nomads (NOH-madz)—people who move from place to place

reservations (rez-ur-VAY-shuhnz)—areas of land set aside for Native Americans to live on

surrendered (suh-REN-durd)—ended a struggle by giving up

travois (tra-VOY)—a frame pulled by a dog or a horse to transport possessions

treaty (TREE-tee)—an agreement or deal that is legally binding on the two or more groups who sign

wickiups (WIK-ee-ups)—dome-shaped Apache homes with a wooden frame covered with bunches of brush or stiff grass

Index

Page numbers in **bold** indicate illustrations

About the Authors

Mark Friedman has been a writer and editor of children's books, textbooks, and other educational materials for more than 15 years. He has written books on U.S. history, countries, holidays, government, poetry, science, and health. Friedman lives in the Chicago area with his wife and daughter.

Peter Benoit is educated as a mathematician but has many other interests. He has taught and tutored high school and college students for many years, mostly in math and science. He also runs summer workshops for writers and students of literature. Benoit has written more than 2,000 poems. His life has been one committed to learning. He lives in Greenwich, New York.